The Journey Of Healing

Richa Chhapolia

BookLeaf
Publishing

India | USA | UK

Made with ❤ on the BookLeaf Publishing Platform

www.bookleafpub.in

www.bookleafpub.com

Dedication

To my husband: Rohit

To my children: Rishi and Yash

To my parents

And to everyone who has faced pain, uncertainty, and slow recovery—may these words bring you comfort, hope, and the courage to keep moving forward.

Preface

Life has a way of testing us when we least expect it. My journey through knee replacement and recovery was one of the most challenging phases of my life, filled with physical pain, emotional turbulence, and moments of deep reflection. But within this journey, I found resilience, gratitude, and a new perspective on life.

This book is not just about healing, it's about rediscovering strength, embracing patience, and finding joy in small victories. Each poem represents a day, a feeling, or a moment that shaped my recovery. Through these verses, I hope to connect with anyone who has ever faced a long road to healing—physically, emotionally, or mentally.

Healing is not just about the body, it's about the mind, heart, and spirit. And if my words can bring comfort or inspiration to even one reader, then my journey has found its purpose beyond just my own recovery.

Acknowledgements

This book wouldn't have been possible without the support of some incredible people in my life.

To my doctor, Dr Sanjay Pai at Apollo Multispeciality Hospital, Jayanagar, Bangalore for giving me the confidence that I can do it and helped me through the step by step post-op recovery.

To my friend Jaya, who not only kept checking on my knee condition much before I even planned to go for the surgery but helped to get connected with Dr Pai and even came to admit me at the hospital on day one.

To my husband Rohit, my biggest motivator, and my constant companion, putting everything else aside to help me heal—this journey would have been impossible without you.

To my children Rishi & Yash, who, despite being miles away, gave me the strength to heal faster, knowing I had to get back on my feet for them.

To my business partner Pooja, who took on extra responsibilities so I could focus solely on my recovery.

To my mother, whose voice, filled with love and warmth, gave me strength whenever I needed it most.

To my father, whose presence in my life makes me feel like a child always cared for and cherished.

To my siblings, whose calls and messages reminded me that I was never alone in this.

To my live-in help Rashmi, who postponed her own plans and stayed just to take care of me—I will always be grateful for your kindness and dedication.

To my cook Radha and house help Mehboobi, who ensured my space was clean, my meals were nutritious, and my needs were met with care.

To my physiotherapists Jack and Priscilla, whose smile and reassurance gave me the hope that I would walk strong again.

To my friends Preeti Jain, Meghna, Manu, Bindu, Sweta, Juhi, Pooja, Reeta, Mitu, Preeti Goel, Raj, Reena bhabhi and to every family member, well-wisher, and reader who has supported me on this journey—thank you for being a part of my healing, my growth, and my story.

This book is as much yours as it is mine.

1. The Walk to the OT

It took me months to say, "Yes, I'll go,"
To brace for the pain, to take it slow.
A restless soul, now forced to stay,
Two, three months—kept at bay.

The hardest step wasn't the knife,
But walking alone to change my life.
The OT doors loomed cold and wide,
A moment where fear sat by my side.

Tears had fallen, silent, deep,
One night, when I could hardly sleep.
I told him, "How will I be alone?"
Yet this battle, I'd fight on my own.

And then? A shift, a sigh, a start—
Pain, yes, but a hopeful heart.
For this pain will heal, unlike before,
And lead me to life—stronger, more.

2. The First Few Days: A Storm Inside

Wrapped in bandages, swollen and tight,
My leg lay heavy—far from right.
Dangling down felt like a dream,
A distant shore, a silent scream.

Bending seemed a wish too tall,
Walking? An idea that felt so small.
Uncertainty whispered in my ear,
"How long till you stand, my dear?"

Then in they walked, calm and sure,
Their voices steady, their promise pure.
"All went well, you'll heal just fine,"
Hope returned—this road was mine.

Pain would stay, but so would grace,
A test of strength I'd learn to face.
And when they said, "Now, take a try,"
I took that step—I won't deny.

3. Homecoming

Under watchful eyes, I learned to stand,
A few slow steps, a guiding hand.
The road ahead was long, I knew,
But home was calling—skies turned blue.

Discharge day, the papers signed,
Excitement swirled within my mind.
No fear, no doubt—just steady grace,
With him beside, my safest place.

The wheels rolled on, the journey back,
Strength in me, no will to lack.
And when my feet first touched our floor,
I walked from the gate to my room once more.

By the temple, I paused to pray,
For all behind and all that lay.
A silent "thank you," deep and true,
For hands that cared and hearts that knew.

My room awaited, soft and neat,
A space of warmth, a place to heal.
Grateful for the love and light,
That made my homecoming feel so right.

4. The Discipline of Healing

One room, one bed, one aching knee,
A journey slow, yet meant to be.
Pain sat beside me, firm and tight,
But I had will, I had fight.

The rules were set, the path was clear,
Recovery asked for grit, not fear.
Three times a day, no meal before,
Until my leg had stretched once more.

The physio came, his words so kind,
Hope like sunlight filled my mind.
Yes, it hurt, but step by step,
I knew this road—I'd not forget.

Beside me stood a steady hand,
A love that chose to understand.
He set the space, he eased the way,
Made sure I'd heal, come what may.

No shortcuts, no looking back,
Discipline kept me on track.
For pain was here, but so was I,
And I would rise—I would fly.

5. The Night That Wouldn't End

The routine was set, all seemed right,
Till I met an endless night.
Eyes wide open, time stood still,
No rest, no dreams, just silent will.

The TV flickered, stories played,
Yet no comfort, no escape made.
Music hummed, soft and deep,
But still, my mind refused to sleep.

Midnight struck—a restless wave,
Something wrong, yet I behaved.
The truth revealed, a simple swap,
The wrong pill took, the right one not.

I wandered slow, from bed to hall,
The walker steady, yet I felt small.
A sofa, a sigh, a desperate shift,

But sleep was a gift I couldn't lift.

He woke up too, scared and lost,
Found me there, no matter the cost.
Beside me, on the couch, he lay,
Holding space till night met day.

No dreams, no peace, just passing time,
Cold and long, that night unkind.
But morning came, as it always must,
And in its light—I placed my trust

6. When Hope Trembled

The morning was bright, the rhythm set,
Each step a promise, no room for regret.
But then he paused, his voice unsure,
A tiny drop—what could it infer?

A message sent, a question raised,
By evening came the waiting phase.
"Come Monday," the doctor said,
Two days of silence, two nights of dread.

At dinner, I sat, my heart weighed down,
My mind a storm, my face a frown.
Just when I thought I'd found my way,
Why did doubt return to stay?

Would this wound betray my trust?
Would my healing turn to dust?
I fought the tears, but they held tight,
A lump of fear, a crack in light.

Then he sat—no rush, no sound,
Just eyes that searched, just love unbound.
His gaze so deep, his worry bare,
A single tear, a whispered prayer.

And in that moment, something turned,
A lesson deep, a truth well-learned.
Pain may come, but so will grace,
Not every trial is a race.

I took a breath, I found my ground,
Held his hand, let strength resound.
"We go ahead," I softly said,
"One step, one day, no fear, no dread."

And so we smiled—though hearts still shook,
For hope, once bent, still never broke.

7. Another Hurdle, Another Fight

The hospital walls, familiar now,
Yet my heart still whispered, asking how.
Wasn't I healing, wasn't I strong?
Why did this road now feel so long?

The doctor spoke, his voice was clear,
"A rare reaction, but no need to fear."
Superficial, yet pain still grew,
Another test, another bruise.

Two more weeks, a slowing tide,
Another weight I held inside.
Frustration knocked, hope grew thin,
Would I ever walk again?

But deep inside, a voice arose,
One I knew, one that knows.
"You've come this far, you'll go beyond,
Pain is tough, but so are you—stay strong."

My husband stood, his steady grace,
A quiet strength, a calming place.
And so I sighed, I wiped my face,
Accepted this unchosen race.

No skipping steps, no turning back,
I'd fight again, despite the lack.
One more battle, one more day,
Still unbroken, come what may.

8. My Business, My Strength

When the world shrank to a single room,
And pain became the loudest tune,
There shone a light, steady and bright,
A purpose that kept me upright.

Not just a name, not just a task,
But a passion that refused to bask.
From bed to phone, from calls to chats,
I found my strength in daily acts.

Orders, messages, plans to make,
A hundred things still at stake.
No time to drown in pain or doubt,
My mind stayed firm, my soul stayed stout.

And in this storm, one stood near,
A partner strong, her support sincere.
Through every hurdle, her hands held tight,
With silent strength, with endless might.

Few even knew the fight I faced,
For work kept sorrow well-embraced.
Each morning rose with hope anew,
A reason to rise, a goal in view.

So while my knees learned how to mend,
My heart stayed whole, my will didn't bend.
For in my work, in what I create,
I found my healing, I shaped my fate.

9. Cookie's Lakshman Rekha

In our home, there's one great rule,
A silent pact, a sacred tool.
No lines were drawn, no locks in sight,
Yet Cookie (Our dog) knew—she must do right.

The queen of hearts, my husband's pet,
So fiercely loyal, no one's threat.
Before my surgery, truth be told,
Her love for him made me feel old!

She'd guard him close, she'd claim her space,
Even I had to fight for my own place!
So when I came back, weak and sore,
I feared she'd leap right through the door.

But oh, the magic in his voice,
One calm command, one simple choice.
"No, Cookie, don't go inside,"
And just like that, she stepped aside.

Now every day, she sits and stares,
Wagging her tail, sending her prayers.
A Lakshman Rekha, firm and true,
A line she'd never dare walk through.

And now the trick has spread around,
If someone seeks peace, safe and sound,
They simply step inside my space—
Cookie won't chase, she knows her place!

Oh, what wisdom, what silent grace,
In her big brown eyes, I see embrace.
Who says only humans know?
Pets understand much more than we show.

10. My Balcony, My World

The world moves fast, yet here I stay,
Watching life unfold each day.
The doors stay shut, but not my mind,
Through my balcony, peace I find.

The golden sun, so warm, so bright,
Whispers hope with morning light.
The moon pours silver, soft and deep,
A quiet promise while I sleep.

The Holika flames rise bold and high,
I watch the sparks kiss the sky.
Laughter drifts from streets below,
Though far, I still feel its glow.

The pool reflects the endless blue,
Its ripples dance with each breeze through.
Children's giggles, footsteps light,
Carry joy from noon to night.

The world outside still calls my name,
Yet healing asks for time and grace.
From this small space, my soul takes flight,
Through endless skies and hopeful light.

11. Conversations That Heal

A ringing phone, a voice so bright,
Lifts my mood, fills me with light.
A simple joke, a loving call,
Reminds me—I'm not alone at all.

Mom checks in, her love so pure,
A mother's voice—a perfect cure.
My mother-in-law, with wisdom deep,
Her words like balm, my heart they keep.

My sister-in-law, a friend so dear,
Her calls bring comfort, wipe a tear.
My business partner, standing tall,
Her strength and faith, I cherish all.

My children, miles away they stay,
Yet close they feel in every way.
Their teasing, love, their daily cheer,
Turn my darkness bright and clear..

Friends drop by, with words so kind,
Moments of joy, pure peace of mind.
We share old tales, we smile, we tease,
Laughter floats upon the breeze.

A gift so rare, yet always free—
Their love, their warmth, their energy.
Though I may heal in solitude,
These voices bring me gratitude.

12. My Silent Strength

Through every ache, through every sigh,
He stood beside, never asking why.
Not once did he falter, not once did he sway,
A pillar of love, come what may.

Day and night, without a pause,
Tending to me, with gentle cause.
A measured step, a steady hand,
His quiet care, a love so grand.

He counted pills, he planned my meals,
Watched my pain, knew how it feels.
With every tear I tried to hide,
He saw it all, he stayed beside.

Leaving his world, his needs, his rest,
Placing me first, giving his best.
No grand gestures, no words so deep,
Just love in action, promises to keep.

I hold his hand, I softly say,
"I'll heal, my love, I'll walk someday."
And when I do, when I stand tall,
I'll know it was him who lifted it all.

13. The Taste of Freedom

Oh, how I miss the open road,
The rush of wheels, the car in mode.
The hum of engines, music loud,
Wind in my hair, free and proud.

The coffee stops, the unplanned turns,
The city lights, the street that burns.
A drive with friends, a late-night spree,
Now just a dream confined to me.

The restaurant buzz, the chai so strong,
Laughter that lingers all night long.
Missing birthdays, missing feasts,
Watching life like a silent priest.

But freedom waits, just down the lane,
This pause is tough, but not in vain.
One day soon, I'll turn the key,
And taste the road that waits for me.

14. Healing in Solitude

Don't call too often, don't wait for long chats,
A healing heart doesn't work like that.
Their day is measured, their steps are slow,
Routine is sacred—let them flow.

A gentle text, a thoughtful line,
Can mean the world, can feel divine.
A joke to laugh, a prayer to send,
A reminder they have a caring friend.

No grand gestures, no endless calls,
Just small kindness—love that falls.
A fruit, a flower, a warm embrace,
Even from afar, can light their space.

A daily text, a thought, a cheer,
Reminds them they are held so near.
No need for visits, no need for fuss,
Just knowing you care is more than enough.

They don't need pity, they don't need tears,
Just faith, just strength to calm their fears.
A silent promise, a steady hand,
That even in stillness, you understand.

15. Gratitude in Every Hand: Part I

Through this long road, rough and steep,
Many hands have held me deep.
Not just in words, not just in prayer,
But in quiet actions, love and care.

My cook arrives, day by day,
Cooking meals in just the right way.
With every bite, strength she restores,
Her kindness lingers, it heals, it pours.

My cleaner comes, twice a day,
Wiping illness, fears away.
Keeping my space fresh and bright,
A shield from germs, a space of light.

My live-in help, so young, so kind,
Put her own dreams behind.
Her wedding waits, yet here she stays,
Holding my world in countless ways.

My physiotherapist, with a hopeful grin,
Pushes me gently, strength within.
Through aching steps, he leads the way,
His smile alone can lift my day.

My business partner, my steady ground,
Handles it all, no complaints, no sound.
"Rest," she says, "I've got this part,"
Her faith in me, a work of art...

16. Gratitude in Every Hand: Part II

My mother's voice, so warm, so bright,
Fills my heart with love and light.
Though miles apart, she's always there,
Her words wrap me in endless care.

And then, my husband, my pillar, my guide,
Never once left my side.
Through every pain, through every tear,
He stayed, he cared, he kept me near.

My in-laws bring the festivals near,
Laughter and warmth, and so much cheer.
They make sure joy still finds its place,
Even in bed, I celebrate with grace.

My children, my heart, though far they roam,
Their love still echoes, guiding me home.
Their pictures near, their voices strong,
They fuel my will to move along.

My sisters call, their voices sweet,
Checking in, making me feel complete.
Their love is steady, a bond so true,
Reminding me—I'll pull through.

My brother, with his daily call,
Lifting me up when I might fall.
With every word, he sets the tone,
"Get up soon, you're not alone."

To every soul, who stood so true,
This heart of mine beats thanks for you.
Not just in words, but in every breath,
You gave me life when I had less.

17. The Road to Recovery

Healing isn't just about time,
It's a battle—both body and mind.
You don't just wait; you take control,
Because recovery is an active role.

You come first—yes, it's true,
Not the chores, not the queue.
Not the guilt of resting still,
Healing takes time, and so it will.

A routine helps, so set it right,
Morning to evening, day to night.
Wake up, move, eat, and rest,
Follow the rhythm—it works best.

Gather your squad, your trusted few,
One for meds, one for food.
One to check, one to care,
Someone who's always aware.

Doctors may say, "This is the way,"
But your body might have its own to say.
Be ready for change, don't lose your grace,
Every recovery has its own pace.

A strong mind speeds a healing hand,
So take a breath, take a stand.
Doubt will creep, pain may stay,
Tell yourself: I'll find my way.

Keep away the noise, the gloom,
Let sunlight brighten up your room.
The world outside can wait a while,
For now, just heal—and do it with a smile.

18. The Day I Take My First Steps Again

The world holds its breath, so do I,
One step forward—I almost fly.
Shaky, slow, but full of grace,
A victory dance in a quiet space.

The ground beneath, once far, now near,
Each step dissolves a hidden fear.
No finish line, no cheering crowd,
Yet my heart beats strong and loud.

A simple walk, a sacred gift,
No longer bound, no longer adrift.
Today I rise, today I stand,
Holding my life in my own hands.

19. The Things I Will Never Take for Granted Again

The touch of grass, the smell of rain,
A stroll outside without the pain.
A sip of chai with friends nearby,
Laughter drifting to the sky.

The morning breeze upon my face,
Moving freely, setting pace.
Holding hands, a warm embrace,
The simple joys I now retrace.

Each moment shines, no longer small,
Life's little gifts—I cherish all.
For what was normal, now feels rare,
And I hold each second with tender care.

20. What Pain Taught Me

Pain is a teacher, slow and wise,
It strips illusions, opens eyes.
It breaks you down, then builds you new,
And shows you strength you never knew.

It teaches patience, breath by breath,
It walks beside you, talks of death.
Yet in its shadows, light appears,
A heart rebuilt through endless tears.

Pain whispered, "Fight," when hope ran thin,
It made me lose, then let me win.
It gave me scars, but left behind,
A soul unshaken, redefined.

21. The Road Ahead—A New Me

I step ahead, a newer me,
Not who I was, but meant to be.
With lessons carved into my soul,
With broken parts that made me whole.

I move with grace, I walk with might,
No rush, no race—just pure delight.
The past was hard, but now I see,
It shaped the best of what's in me.

Ahead, the road is wide and bright,
With dreams reborn in golden light.
A life once paused, now moves along,
With love, with hope, with heart, with song.

I wear my scars like crown of gold,
Each tells a tale of strength untold.
Not just survived - I chose to grow,
A warrior's heart , a soul that glows.

With every step, my spirit soars,
Unbound, alive - forevermore.